# Children...

## Why Not Raise Them?

All rights reserved. This book is licensed for your personal use. This book or any portion thereof may not be reproduced or used in any manner whatsoever without the express written permission of the publisher except for the use of brief quotations in a book review. Send those requests via email to FordPublishingGroup@Gmail.com

For information about special discounts for bulk purchases or to book an event, please contact the publisher at FordPublishingGroup@Gmail.com

**Copyright © 2018 Darlene Ford**

This book was published and printed in the United States.

**ISBN~13: 978-0-692-06977-6**

*Dedicated to the Lord for all He is in my life!*

# ACKNOWLEDGEMENTS

I thank God for giving me the words and knowledge to write this book and for loving me enough to allow me to give a little of my wisdom in hopes to help others grow!

I would like to thank my cousin Dee Fulton for believing in me and supporting me with financial support.

I would like to thank Dorene Bratton, Charlesann Goode, Lorene Edwards, Cathy Currence and Selina Davie for praying me through and for all the great support while I wrote and asked many questions while writing.

I am forever thankful for the support from my now deceased brother JC Smarr, Jr. who was a strong influence in my life and James Smarr for the beautiful photo of me. I especially would like to thank my children Shanda Ford and Marteshia Ford-Funderburk for blessing me with grandchildren who really helped me in making decisions to write this book and for all your encouragement and support in pressing me on!

# CHAPTER ONE

*Two or Six or More! OH MY!*

**R**AISING CHILDREN TO TRUST GOD and to be respectful in this day and time can be and is a challenge. But we can do it. Children are a handful to raise these days because there is so much peer pressure facing them on a daily basis. On top of that, there are many different standards by which young parents are raising their children. **Young parents use various disciplinary standards. Some may spank, some may not, or some may think spanking is too harsh. Some may use timeout. Time out may not work for other parents.** As a parent, ask yourself, "By what standard am I raising my child?" Am I raising them to work for the Lord or work the streets?

Being a parent raising a child today, is nothing compared to–what parenting was when I was a young girl. As a child, I was taught to respect my parents, my teachers, the elderly and those in authority. I also had respect for myself.

## Teach our children to respect and love the Lord

First, we must teach our children to love the Lord. As they see you praying and hear you say, "I will trust the Lord for what we need," they too will learn and know where their help will come from. Teach them to respect the authority of teachers, preachers, and other adults. Showing them how the Holy Spirit lives in your life will help them let the Holy Spirit into their lives as well; and He, the Holy Spirit, can also help them to make right decisions just like He helps parents to make right decisions in their lives.

Teach your children to say thank you to people who give them gifts, clothes or other things. For example, some children only call their absent parent when they need or want something. Children should be allowed and encouraged to call the absent parent just to talk about school, a field trip they went on, or when something is on their mind. This avenue of communication creates opportunities for that absent parent to put in much needed time with their child and help him or her to develop a healthy and long-lasting relationship with that parent.

As cautious parents, we are aware that some authority figures do not respect the innocence of a child. Therefore, we teach them if it doesn't look right or if it doesn't feel right, don't do it. Then, be sure to tell them to tell someone that they trust about the incident. We teach our children not to let anyone touch them on any part of their body where they don't want to be touched.

Teaching a child what it means to obey the rules may take some time. We have to be careful how we approach them. We don't want to be seen as monsters to them, but we want them to understand that discipline must be a part of their upbringing. Never let your children get away with disrespecting you, whether at home or in public. Teach them to respect you at all times. "Children obey your parents in the Lord for this is right. Honor thy father and mother, which is the first commandment with promise; that it may be well with thee, and thou mayest live long on the earth" (Ephesians 6:1-3). It is during these teaching moments that we can teach them the meaning of Ephesians 6:3.

If you tell a child to do something, you need to remember that they are not little adults. They are children. We tell them to hang up their clothes, but we haven't taught or shown them how. It is our responsibility to show our children the how-to's of the home.

**Raising a Child with Behavioral Problems**

Have you ever wondered, "Is this a bad child?" Well, **maybe, maybe not.** It may be that what that child needs is more adult hugs and attention at that moment. As a parent, I wasn't always there for my children due to working a full time and sometimes a part time job. I just believe that they needed more love, time and hugs from me. Parents sometime make it hard for children to express themselves. It is critical that we help that child who has behavioral problems while he or she is young. Once that child gets to the age of independence, they will freeze up and not want to talk to you about their problem. Train them right and train them well, now! These are children that one day may have to take care of us.

# CHILDREN...WHY NOT RAISE THEM?

**Two questions to ask yourself as a parent:**

- What would I do if I couldn't do for myself?

- If it becomes necessary in the future, will this child that I'm raising be ready or responsible enough to take care of me?

# CHAPTER TWO

*"I Love You."*

## DON'T BE AFRAID TO SAY THESE WORDS

IT IS GREAT TO TELL YOUR CHILDREN you love them. They need to hear this coming out of your mouth often. How else will they learn to say the words? We give our children expensive things, but not love. Talk to your child – really talk. Have a special time to talk to all of them together and talk to them one-on-one.

Remember that each child is different. Never, ever compare one child to another sibling. You may have one child that does well on everything and another that needs help. Remember that children are gifts from the Lord. "Lo, children are a heritage of the LORD: and the fruit of the womb is his reward" (Psalms 127:3). God gave them to us for the good times and the bad times. Some children are stronger willed than others.

You will be able to distinguish the child that will rebel against everything you say. So, what do you do?

# CHILDREN...WHY NOT RAISE THEM?

First, PRAY! Next, always keep the line of communication open with that child and be ready to talk whenever that child is ready to talk. If he or she doesn't willingly talk, you may have to begin by randomly asking questions. The child may begin to feel comfortable and start talking to you. Dealing with a strong-willed child can be difficult, but you must be determined to overpower that child's will (with love), so that you can help them through what they are experiencing at that moment. Keep reminding yourself that these children will someday become adults, and if they are not talking to you and expressing themselves at a young age, they will have difficulty doing so as a youth or as adults.

**Hugs Are Great**

You can show love to your boy or girl by hugging them. Hugs make a child feel secure and safe. Hugs can make a child smile even after just being punished for a wrong doing. Allowing a child to hug you can also bring joy where there once was sorrow. So never reject a hug from your child. A genuine hug also sends an important message to a child that might be necessary following a serious confrontation. It tells your children that you still love them dearly. Hugs can take some of the sting out of loud words that were intended to help and not hurt.

# Darlene Ford

**What A Hug Tells You About Your Child and/or Yourself:**

- I love you.

- "Your hair looks a little oily today, Sweetie. A good shampoo before bed will probably help that, don't you think?"

- With a warm smile and a hug, you can give your child a reminder: "Don't forget to brush your teeth before you go to bed."

- Hugs let the children know they are loved whether they are right or wrong.

- A gentle hug can take some sting out when you ask, "Did you use deodorant after your bath today?

- Hugs soften the atmosphere when private/serious conversations are necessary - such as confirming whether or not the child has head lice.

Parents, you may have one child that will not come to you for hugs. This will be the child that you will have to approach first to give a hug. Don't forget that child. Some children don't express themselves like other children. Pay close attention to their individual needs.

I remember myself as being a very quiet child. I kept everything inside, never expressing what I really felt. I have vivid memories of times when my sister ran to daddy for hugs when he came home from work. I was so shy that I sat still and withdrew even though all the while I was saying within myself, "I want a hug, too!" However, not being an outgoing child, I instead just sat there feeling left out. I'm just now at the stage of my life where I'm outspoken

## CHILDREN...WHY NOT RAISE THEM?

enough to ask for what I need or want. If you can identify with what I'm saying here, start making changes in your family life now.

So, what am I saying? It is vital that you keep your eyes open to all your children's needs. As my two girls were growing up, I saw some of the same traits in them that my sister and I had when we were growing up. Some of the changes that needed to be made, unfortunately, were not made. I didn't have an opportunity or didn't know everything that I needed to know, to make the necessary changes. That was it. I didn't know what to do or how to do it to make those changes. My parents didn't see the withdrawn me, so they didn't even know that I needed help. I also see some of the same traits in my grandchildren. I hope as you read this book it will not be too late for you, your children, and the generations to come.

If you are a working parent, and your children are in school, they've been away from you all day. When your children come home, they want some Mamma and Daddy time. Because you have to get dinner on the table, clothes washed, and things ready for the next day, it might be all too easy to forget to spend some time with your children.

I learned to set aside some time for my children while I cooked. My children sat at the dinner table and did their homework. I was able to hear about school and also help them with their homework while trying not to complain about the note or sad face on their school papers.

While multi-tasking, I always made it a point to remember that children are not another chore. Children need your time before you start your household duties. Talk to them and find out what they did in school; or just

# Darlene Ford

talk to them in general. Sometimes we just need to hear what they are saying to us.

# CHAPTER THREE

*Give Respect – Get Respect*

IN MY YEARS OF PARENTING and grand parenting, I have found that if you don't teach respect to your children they will not have respect for themselves or for others. It really is okay for you to respect them for who they are as children, and in complete confidence of knowing that you are teaching them respect for one another. As parents, we should respect our children's privacy. However, if a child tends to get into trouble a lot, we must make sure that child is not left alone behind closed bedroom doors. A child's idle hands behind closed doors present an opportunity for mischievous behavior. That could create an opportunity for the child to watch a movie that they should not be watching.

Instead of allowing your children to be away from your presence by themselves too long, have a conversation with your child. Find out how they are doing. Talking to them to find out if anything is going on that they may need to discuss. Allow them some time behind closed doors. The door should be open more than closed. Take some time and not allow the child to babysit themselves.

Take it from me, a surprise visit into your child's room every now and then is good. I try to take every chance I get to be with my child, to talk and spend time with them. The Message Bible says, "We should not get too busy that you can't spend some time with the child to keep him from mischievous activity" (Ephesians 5:15). Too much separation between you and your child creates a barrier of division. A child behind closed door can also give an impression of division. Instead, try to know this child's interests. Then make time for him or her, and a genuine effort for you and that child to get together sometime and do those things together.

Just saying, "Because I said so" is not enough. In the early stages of their lives, begin teaching and training your child how to respect things such as their clothes, room, books, food, church, school, and each other.

In 2004, I was the 49-year-old grandmother of eight grandchildren – six girls and two boys (my little angels). I've had all of them at the house at one time and I tell you, they were a handful. I found that they all wanted my attention, sometimes all at the same time. I had to figure out a way to tell one child to hold on for a few minutes while I addressed the needs of the other child without hurting that child's feelings. At the same time, I needed to listen attentively to the one child talk. When one child is excitedly talking to you and all the other children want to talk to you at that same time, this is an opportunity to teach them to take turns. I did not want to hurt one child's feelings by telling them to be quiet. You want to show them respect by teaching

# CHILDREN…WHY NOT RAISE THEM?

them to wait until their turn comes for your attention. By doing this, you are also teaching them respect for each other. We need to respect their need for attention and find a way to spend time with them, and this will help them learn how to respect others.

# CHAPTER FOUR

**Parents Give Each Child a Chore**

*Assigning Household Chores*

**I BELIEVE EACH CHILD NEEDS** an assigned chore to do around the house. Even a two-year-old needs to pick up their toys and put them in the toy box after they have finished playing with them. After your child has done his or her chore, reward them with a smile and the pleasure of hearing your voice affirming them by saying, "Well done!" or "Great job!" This will encourage the child to do that same chore without being told to do it, and will teach that child how to take care of their things and those of others.

Some parents with multiple children may have to wash clothes four to six times a week. Letting your children help with these chores around the house will help them understand what chores are all about. For example: a family of six children and one or two parents will change clothes every day. That equals at least six pair of pants, six pairs of underwear, six pair of socks, and six shirts and/or blouses. Then there will be six or eight bath towels. Sounds like a wash day to me!

Don't forget the trash! You may need to empty your trash every day and sometimes twice a day. Likewise, you will wash dishes two to three times a day, sweep the floor two or three times a day and also mop the floor two times a day (depending on the age of the children). Children love to help wash dishes at an early age.

**Babysitter**

Sometimes it is necessary to leave the younger children with an older child. But, we have to remember not to make this an everyday thing. Remember, these are your children and they are your responsibility.

Never make the oldest child a fulltime baby sitter of the younger children. They will end up resenting them or the other children will end up resenting the older child. Occasionally it is acceptable if the older child is over the age of 12. This will also help teach job skills, for later. However, they will have to first learn from you. Plus, they will need to know how to find you if they need to while babysitting.

# CHAPTER FIVE

*Parents and Discipline*

CHILDREN NEED DISCIPLINE, BUT NOT for everything they do or did wrong. If we fail to discipline our children and have occasions where we need or expect someone else to babysit them, we would be doing the babysitter an injustice. It really is our responsibility to teach them to respect others and the things of others. My grandchildren say that I have too many rules in my house, but I let them know without hesitancy, that rules are meant to keep the house in order. Then, I explain each rule to them when the time arises to enforce that rule.

# CHILDREN...WHY NOT RAISE THEM?

**Here are a few simple rules that help my grandchildren keep my house in order:**

- Don't jump on the furniture.
- Put trash in the trash can, not in the yard or on the floor.
- Pick up your toys and put them back in their designated places.

I found it best to enforce rules on the spot. You cannot instruct a four or six-year-old child not to put their feet in the chair until he or she actually puts their feet in the chair. You can only enforce a rule once that action becomes a reality. Little children are too young to remember every rule we give them.

Parents not agreeing on how to raise their children can confuse the child. Both parents should agree on the decisions made, then address the child so that child will understand what to do the next time something comes up that they do not understand.

Raising our children was hard sometimes because their father and I could not agree on what to tell our children, and how to explain anything to our two girls. We also could not agree on whether the girls should have understood the first time we told them. However, I believe that if parents explain things to children so that they understand the reasons why they should not do a thing again, the children will understand what to do the next time a problem arises. At some point, you may feel like you tell your children things over and over again and they never use what they've been told. Keep teaching and training them because one day (and it may not be until near adulthood) you will see the evidence of all of your hard but loving work in them.

# Darlene Ford

**Parents, Establish a Set Bedtime**

Setting a specific bedtime for children will allow for parental personal time. It will also teach them how to organize their own life as adults by getting the rest they need. Putting my children to bed at a specific time played a large part in my life. I was able to get things done that I was not able to do while spending time with them. If you are married, **do not** forget that you and your husband will need time for each other, time for the Lord, and time to plan the next day's events or activities. Single parents, you will also want some time for yourself and time to talk to the Lord. A set bedtime is best for both the children and for the parents.

# CHAPTER SIX

*Who is Our Children's Role Model?*

**D**O NOT LET YOUR CHILDREN model themselves after someone other than you. You are the best role model your child could ever pattern themselves after. I was the youngest girl of five children with a mother and father in the home.

My father worked three jobs (one full time and two part-time). My mother worked cleaning the homes of others. My parents taught us respect. When the adults had a conversation, the children were not allowed to be in the same room with the adults. We had to leave the room and go play while they talked.

In this day and age, we have lost the family time at the dinner table. When I was growing up we gathered as a family for dinner. We had table manners and we knew how to take care of the things that we had; few as they may have been. We were responsible for specific chores around the house. We had to wash dishes, clean our room, mop and wax the hardwood floors, polish the silverware, and bring coal and wood from outside to heat the house. Yes, in the sixties, as we got older, we had to cook. We did not talk back to our parents and we did not disrespect them.

I taught my girls to knock on the bedroom door before they entered. That taught them the value of privacy. Mothers, there is an urgency that we teach our girls not to wear their dresses or skirts too short. Their tops should not be cut too low at the breast. Teach our girls that their breasts or the cleavage of their breasts should not be on display for anyone to see except their husband. **This will help them to have respect for their bodies.**

Fathers, it is of the utmost importance that our boys pull their pants up. Teach your sons how to respect girls at an early age. Teach them that it is still okay to open the door for a girl. If you begin by showing them that you, in fact, do open the door for their mother, they will follow your lead and do the same.

Mothers, if **you do not** have a husband in the home to teach your sons, then you must take on that responsibility and teach them. Hitting your son in the chest is not going to make him a man. Teaching him to be a man will make him a man. Your children are looking at you, whether you see it or not.

Children naturally watch their parents and learn from what they see them doing and how they are talking. They learn the right that a parent does. They also learn, unfortunately, the wrong that parents do! Remember that the next time you are doing something.

No, parenting did not come with a Parent's Manual, but you can stand, teach, and train your children based on the word of God. "And ye fathers provoke not your children to wrath: but bring them up in the nurture and admonition of the Lord" **(Ephesians 6:4)**.

# CHAPTER SEVEN

*Parents Do Not Be Afraid to Say No*

TEACH YOUR CHILDREN THAT "NO" means no. I did not understand all of the 'no's' that came my way as a child; no child really does. However, when I became a parent, I began to understand more and more. Believe me; it will all come back to your remembrance. Once you say "no," do not change your mind as this will only confuse the child. We must be consistent.

Never go backward and forward. Example: establish a specific bedtime, homework time, and Bible study time. Once you do that stay with it. It will teach your child consistency. Of course, there may be times when **it may be necessary for you to change your decision because of unforeseen reasons** - reasons that may be totally out of your control. Just be sure to let the child know that they will have to go back to the regular way of doing things

# CHILDREN…WHY NOT RAISE THEM?

As parents, we need to know our children and try to recognize their needs. No one can know all of their children's needs. I did not know all my children's needs. Not knowing may cause problems in the long run.

I went through my girls' book bags to see if there were any school papers that needed to be signed. Sometimes a child will forget to give you their school papers – children do forget sometimes, just as we do. Never assume they will remember everything you tell them. You may have to repeat rules over and over again to your child until they become young adults. Then you will see the fruit of your labor.

Sometimes it is necessary to explain to the child why they cannot have something, do something, or go somewhere. Parents, remember the word of God is your best source of explanation. The time will come when your child has matured and reached the point of asking adult questions. How will you respond? What will you say?

In the King James Version of the Bible, the word of God says, "Now, concerning the things whereof ye wrote unto me: It is good for a man not to touch a woman. Nevertheless, to avoid fornication, let every man have his own wife, and let every woman have her own husband" (1 Corinthians 7:1-3).

It is my personal belief that explaining some things to a child will help the child understand and learn to apply those things. How else will a child learn if you as a responsible adult will not explain to them how things are done? When you say to your child, "Just say no," you need to explain what that means. Don't just tell your children, "Don't smoke." Tell them why not. Don't just say to your children, "Don't have sex before you get married." Tell them

# Darlene Ford

why they shouldn't. As parents, there are some things that we really just need to explain. You must also live what you are explaining. Your lifestyle should line up with your explanation.

# CHAPTER EIGHT

*Children Come First*

Parents, I am a firm believer that some of the things we want for ourselves may need to be put on hold just for a little while, so that we can get the things our children need. If someone wants to gift you money to take care of some of your needs, let them know that you may use some of that gift to buy something specific that you know your child needs. Don't put expensive or unnecessary things before your children's needs. After the Lord, children come first.

**Financial Teaching (Proverbs)**

Let us teach our child about money. Teach them that money is not and will not be their friend if they don't handle it correctly. "For the love of money is the root of all kinds of evil. And some people, craving money, have wandered from the true faith and pierced themselves with many sorrows" (1 Timothy 6:9-11). Help your children to understand that money was made to

# Darlene Ford

pay for things as you purchase them. Teach them not to use plastic (credit cards). I don't care what people may say about it, have only one credit card for emergencies. **The card can be paid off each month, with the understanding that credit cards draw interest and makes it harder to pay off.** There should be no money emergencies if we teach our children about money at an early age. I was not the one to teach my girls about money. We had little and they did not get an allowance but once in a while. When you give your child an allowance, teach tithing to give back the ten percent to the Lord according to Malachi 3:10 -11 which says, "Bring ye all the tithes into the storehouse, that there may be meat in mine house, and prove me now herewith, saith the Lord of hosts, if I will not open you the windows of heaven, and pour you out a blessing, that there shall not be room enough to receive it. And I will rebuke the devourer for your sakes, and he shall not destroy the fruits of your ground: neither shall your vine cast her fruit before the time in the field, saith the Lord of hosts." We go a step further and teach them to give ten percent to the Lord, save ten percent for themselves, and then use the rest as needed.

I was in debt when I had my first child, when I got married, and when I had my second child. We could not pay our bills on time and we did not have the option of giving an allowance to our children on a regular basis. The bible tells us we are the child's first teachers. "Train up a child in the way he should go and when he is old he will not depart from it" (Proverbs 22:6).

# CHAPTER NINE

*Mothers Go With Your First Intuition*

I used to dream about my girls and most of the time that dream would let me know that they had already done something wrong, or they would before the week was out. That's a special gift that God gives to mothers. Use that with which the Lord has blessed you. **We as parents can use that gift as a blessing from the** Lord. Know your children's friends up close and personal. In other words, you don't need to hand pick your child's friends, but take the time to get to know their friends. Children will not tell you everything, so you will need to ask questions. If you begin teaching them early in their life the things I have said in this book, they will pick the right friends to be around.

If you have a special child in your home (one who may not learn at the same pace as the other children), be sure to take extra time out with that child and help them to learn.

# Darlene Ford

**Grandparents and the Role We Play**

Grandparents, we are grandparents, not free babysitters. It really is ok to say "no" to our children. I believe grandparents are to help out when we can and keep the grandchildren once in a while, not every weekend or when your children are tired themselves from working or staying out too late. Remember, you too have a life and your son or daughter should not expect you to take on the job of raising their children (a job you have already done for them when they were children). We have already raised our children and we shouldn't have to raise our grandchildren. Obviously, there could be situations or extenuating circumstances where there would be reasons why you would raise a grandchild. That's different. However, we should not feel bad when we have to say "no, not today." Once our own children have gotten to the age of leaving the nest, we must let them go, believing that all the training, all the love, and most importantly the power of the Holy Spirit, will take them and keep them.

As a child, my daddy would not let us go out to a lot of places. I used to say (to myself of course), "Why can't I go to the ballgames with my friends?" Or, "Why can't I spend the night out with my friend?" Daddy was a hard man, but I want you to know that I really appreciate it now. Children will not understand all the things their parents will say. But in the long run they will understand the reason of it all. Even though I did things in my life that I knew were not right, I came around and remembered what I was taught. I can truly say that I am not on drugs today nor am I a drunkard, thanks to the teachings in my home.

# CHILDREN...WHY NOT RAISE THEM?

There are young girls and young ladies today that just do not seem to care about themselves or their future. That must change. In this time of such an awareness of AIDS and all the other things that cannot be cured, it should be a given that our young girls would keep themselves pure. You would even think that the young men would keep themselves pure. The bible tells us that our body is the temple of God. If our body is the temple of God, then we should keep it beautiful and clean. We as parents must teach our children how to live. We need to make them understand what God says about the body. We must teach our children how to live God's way. Once a baby is born and placed in the arms of his mother, that is the first day of training. A baby knows when Momma is holding him or her how Momma is feeling. If the Mother is having a bad day and she picks up her baby, the baby will feel what the mother is feeling. There is an old saying that we don't come with a book of instructions. Nevertheless, we have the roadmap of life – the BIBLE.

We just have to take one day at a time and learn as we go. We very well may not come with a written book of instructions; however, wisdom is our best teacher. We need to hear from our older mothers who have already raised children. They have already gone through situations that the younger mothers may be going through. Although some of the older mothers may have made mistakes, they can still pull from those mistakes and show and tell the younger mothers what to do, and what not to do.

None of us are perfect, but we can all learn from each other.

# Reference Scriptures

Ephesians 6:1-3

Ephesians 5:15 The Message Bible

Ephesians 6:4

Psalms 127:3

1 Corinthians 7:1-3

Malachi 3:10-11

Proverbs 22:6

www.ingramcontent.com/pod-product-compliance
Lightning Source LLC
Chambersburg PA
CBHW060622070426
42449CB00042B/2462